GALAXY OF SUPERSTARS

98°
Ben Affleck
Jennifer Aniston
Backstreet Boys
Brandy
Garth Brooks
Mariah Carey
Matt Damon
Cameron Díaz
Leonardo DiCaprio
Céline Dion
Sarah Michelle Gellar
Tom Hanks
Hanson
Jennifer Love Hewitt
Faith Hill
Lauryn Hill
Jennifer Lopez
Ricky Martin
Ewan McGregor
Mike Myers
'N Sync
Gwyneth Paltrow
LeAnn Rimes
Adam Sandler
Will Smith
Britney Spears
Spice Girls
Jonathan Taylor Thomas
Venus Williams

CHELSEA HOUSE PUBLISHERS

GALAXY OF SUPERSTARS

Sarah Michelle Gellar

Marilyn D. Anderson

CHELSEA HOUSE PUBLISHERS
Philadelphia

Frontis: Best Known for the title role in the television series *Buffy the Vampire Slayer*, Sarah Michelle Gellar has begun to branch out into feature films.

CHELSEA HOUSE PUBLISHERS

Editor in Chief: Sally Cheney
Associate Editor in Chief: Kim Shinners
Production Manager: Pamela Loos
Art Director: Sara Davis

Produced by
21st Century Publishing and Communications, Inc.
New York, New York
http://www.21cpc.com

The Chelsea House World Wide Web address is
http://www.chelseahouse.com

First Printing

1 3 5 7 9 8 6 4 2

Library of Congress Cataloging-in-Publication Data

Anderson, Marilyn D.
Sarah Michelle Gellar / Marilyn D. Anderson.
p. cm. — (Galaxy of superstars)
Includes bibliographical references and index.
Summary: A biography of the young actress who has been seen on the soap opera, "All My Children" and as the star in "Buffy the Vampire Slayer."
ISBN 0-7910-6461-1 (alk. paper)
1. Gellar, Sarah Michelle, 1977– —Juvenile literature. 2. Actors—United States—Biography—Juvenile literature. [1. Gellar, Sarah Michelle, 1977– . 2. Actors and actresses. 3. Women—Biography.] I. Title. II. Series.

PN2287.G46 A53 2001
792'.028'092—dc21
[B] 2001042096

CONTENTS

1

THE BIG WIN

The year is 1995 and Sarah Michelle Gellar, barely 18, is spending this May evening at television's Daytime Emmy Awards ceremony instead of at her prom. Wearing a beautiful, white designer gown, she waits with other popular stars to see who will win television's highest award.

Just arriving in a limousine and being with the rich and famous would be exciting enough for most young women, but Sarah is used to all this. She has been a major player on the set of *All My Children* since February 1993 and was nominated for an Emmy herself in 1994.

Sarah wasn't disappointed when she failed to win in 1994. After all, she had only been playing the role of "Kendall" for a year, and Susan Lucci, the leading lady of *All My Children*, had been nominated 14 times without success.

But things were different in 1995. This year Sarah knew she had a chance of taking home the prize. The part on *All My Children* had been a big step forward for Sarah, and it had also been a logical one. Twelve years earlier she had appeared as a flower girl on *Guiding Light*, another daytime program. More recently she had starred as the rich and spoiled Sydney Rutledge in a short-lived daytime series called *Swans Crossing*.

Sarah Michelle Gellar proudly displays her Daytime Emmy Award for her role as Kendall in *All My Children*.

When Sarah's agent told her to read for the part of Kendall, no one seemed to know much about the role. It might call for just a few walk-ons or the character might become a regular on the show.

As it turned out, Kendall was a much bigger role than Sarah thought. The producers of *All My Children* were looking for someone to play the long-lost daughter of the series' main character, Erica Kane, played by Susan Lucci. Since Erica was one of the cruelest and most complex characters on daytime television, Kendall was supposed to be able to show the same character traits. They thought Kendall should be about 23 years old, and they expected to hire an actress in her twenties.

But Sarah, only 15 at the time, quickly impressed everyone with her ability. Casting director Judy Wilson said later, "As soon as Sarah walked in the door, I knew she was something special. She has that combination of possessing terrific range, being adorable, and having a little spice."

A few days later Sarah was thrilled to hear that she had won the part. She said in an interview with Michael Rush of *Daytime TV* in 1993, "[W]hen they told me I would be playing her [Susan Lucci's] daughter, I was like 'I'm her what?! Daughter? Me?!'"

Sarah was nervous about going to her first rehearsal. "I kept thinking 'what if I'm really bad and they fire me?'" But the experienced stars of *All My Children* quickly put her at ease. She said, "When I walked into the rehearsal hall, Susan and Michael [Nader] were rehearsing a scene and I just snuck in the back and tried to blend in with the coffee machine, when all of a sudden, Susan said,

In 1993, 15-year-old Sarah Michelle Gellar was cast as Kendall, Susan Lucci's daughter on *All My Children*. Sarah won a Daytime Emmy Award for her role in 1995.

'Hold it, we need to stop for a minute,' and she walked over to me and said, 'Congratulations! I'm very glad you're here' and introduced me to everyone who was there. She really helped me and always made sure I was okay during my first couple of weeks."

Sarah's character, Kendall, lost no time in shaking things up. Just as Erica was about to get married to her true love, Dmitri, the mysterious young Kendall arrived in town. At first Kendall appeared to idolize Erica, but she refused to tell anyone about her past.

Then Erica's beloved daughter Bianca got hurt in a riding accident, and Kendall finally told Erica that she, too, was Erica's daughter. Kendall was the child that Erica gave birth to after being raped when she was 14, the child that Erica then gave up for adoption. Erica had been trying to forget about this unhappy experience. So, rather than having a happy reunion with her long-lost mother, Kendall faced rejection and vowed to get even.

Sarah loved her part. She later said of the experience, "It was amazing playing a psycho-loony. . . . It was *great*. In the first month alone, I tried to seduce my stepfather, burned my parents' divorce papers, slept with a stable boy, and got arrested."

Sarah quickly made friends with other talented kids on the set. One of those friends was Lindsey Price, who played An Li. From Sarah's first day on *All My Children*, Lindsey was there to give her support, and the show's other actors and actresses became like a family to her.

Watching veteran actors and actresses work taught Sarah valuable lessons about her craft. In the beginning, she admired Susan Lucci just as Kendall had admired Erica. A 1994 interview quoted Sarah as saying of Lucci, "I'm always worried about where I'm going to stand and what I'm going to say, and she does it effortlessly."

In 1999 she told Hugh Hart of *Ultimate TV*, "Daytime [television] played a huge role in developing my craft. You learn how to hit a mark [an x on the floor marking where the actor is supposed to stand] and how not to shadow somebody [get in that person's light]. So when you get a prime time show, you can really concentrate on the emotions and not worry about the technical [side]."

The job of a soap opera star was not all fun and games. It was hard work with long hours and lots of pressure. Since *All My Children* was aired daily, the cast had very little time to get each segment on tape. Every day there was a thick new script for Sarah to memorize. She would rehearse her scenes once or twice, and

Sarah gained valuable experience working with Susan Lucci and other veteran actors on *All My Children*. In 1995, Sarah left the show to pursue her acting career in Los Angeles.

then the cameras started rolling. If she didn't get it right on the first try, it had better be perfect on the second, because there was no time to waste.

Susan Lucci was wonderful to Sarah at the beginning, but that apparently didn't last. Soon rumors were flying about a major feud between the two. Sources told Danna Kennedy of *Entertainment Weekly* (*EW*) that it all started when one of the directors told Sarah she needed to "punch up" a certain scene that she had with Lucci. Unfortunately Lucci hadn't heard this conversation, so when Sarah came on stronger in the next take, Lucci supposedly accused Sarah of trying to upstage her.

From then on, Lucci, it was said, was as nasty toward Sarah as Erica Kane was toward Kendall. *EW* reported that for a six-week period, Lucci refused to be in the same scene with Sarah. *EW* also said that during this time no publicity materials were allowed to be sent out that had the two women in the same picture.

Many thought that Sarah's Emmy nomination in 1994 had something to do with this treatment. They believed that Lucci was jealous of Sarah and felt threatened by how quickly the young star was nominated for this award. Although Sarah was careful not to say what she really thought, reporters gleefully wrote unflattering stories about Lucci's miserable behavior toward Sarah, other costars, and one of her hairdressers.

Now it was time for the 1995 awards ceremony. Sarah tried to stay out of Susan Lucci's way and enjoy herself with the younger stars of the series. She tried not to think about whether or not she would win an Emmy.

The host of this nationally broadcast NBC program had already introduced dozens of famous celebrities who had presented dozens of awards. Directors, producers, writers, make-up artists, film editors, costumers, people in charge of lighting, and camera experts filed across the stage to pick up the coveted golden statues.

It was now time for the "Outstanding Younger Leading Actress in a Drama Series" award. The nominees were: "Sarah Michelle

Gellar as Kendall in *All My Children,* Kimberly Anderson McCullough as Robin in *General Hospital,* Rachel Miner as Michelle in *The Guiding Light,* and Heather Tom as Victoria in the *Young and the Restless.* The envelope please. . . ."

The room was quiet. Sarah held her breath as the presenter opened the envelope . . . "and the winner is . . . Sarah Michelle for Kendall on *All My Children.*"

The audience exploded into applause. The band began to play as Sarah's friends hugged and kissed her. She walked proudly to the podium to accept the Emmy and thank everyone who helped her on the road to success.

The Emmy came early in Sarah's career, but it still holds a special place in her heart. Years later she was to say, "[F]or me, the Emmy was a validation of the work that I'd done and the time that I spent there [in New York]. But at the same time, I was ready to move on." Indeed, within weeks of the award, Sarah left *All My Children* and was on her way to Los Angeles to take the next step in her life and her career.

2

GETTING STARTED

Sarah Michelle Gellar was born in New York City on April 14, 1977, and for most of her early years she lived in an apartment on Manhattan's Upper East Side. Her mother Rosellen was a kindergarten teacher, and to this day Sarah calls her "the most amazing woman that I've ever met and probably will ever meet in my entire life."

Sarah's biological father, Steven, left in 1984, when she was only seven. It was 10 years before her mother remarried a wonderful man who enjoyed attending Sarah's school programs. In the years between, Sarah and Rosellen struggled to make ends meet, and Sarah learned the value of money. She says, "If we couldn't make the rent, I knew. If we were in trouble, I knew."

Even before her father left, Sarah began to help pay the bills. When she was only four, the adorable, dark-haired little girl and her mother were eating in a restaurant "that was a showcase for young kids. I, of course, was getting up there and singing for no apparent reason. Anyway, an agent came up to me and said, 'Do you want to be on television?'" Her mother just laughed it off.

So Sarah took matters into her own hands. She had

Sarah's mother, Rosellen, allowed her to take a few commercial and movie roles when she was very young. Soon, Sarah's career as a young actress began to take off.

just learned how to give her name, address, and phone number "in case I got kidnapped." She gave the agent all the information she needed to call Sarah's house about a week later. Rosellen hung up on the agent the first time, but later she agreed to let her daughter audition for some television commercials and movie roles.

A week after that phone call, Sarah was sent to read for a part as Valerie Harper's daughter in a television movie called *An Invasion of Privacy.* The casting people wanted Sarah to read with Harper, but the star had already left the set when Sarah got there. This was not a problem for Sarah. She proceeded to read her own lines as well as Harper's, which she did in a lower voice. Sarah was hired on the spot.

The main thing she remembers about making this movie was being cold and there being lots of snow. In fact, she claims she was so small and the drifts so deep that someone had to carry her around to be sure she wouldn't sink out of sight.

Modeling jobs with the famous Wilhemina agency and more than 100 television commercials followed. Sometimes the hours were long and the work was hard for such a young girl, but Sarah was quickly becoming a professional. Once, she remembers, "I had to open up a closet door and hundreds and thousands of these little cotton balls were supposed to fall out on top of me. . . . I just couldn't pull the door open, and I just stood there until they had to stop shooting and fix the door."

Another time, for a Shake 'n Bake commercial, she did the same scene over so many times that she had to eat "98 pieces of chicken."

Her worst experience with commercials was when a series of Burger King spots landed her in court. The script had Sarah saying that McDonald's hamburgers were 20 percent smaller than Burger King's hamburgers. In those days, however, rival companies did *not* mention the competition by name. McDonald's was so upset that they sued everyone involved, including little Sarah. The suit was later settled out of court.

When she got to appear on *Late Night with David Letterman* over this battle of the burgers, she said that birthday parties at McDonald's were a big problem for her. Even though she was only five years old, she always had to wear a big hat and sunglasses to avoid being recognized.

In 1984 Sarah once again had the opportunity to appear in a film. This time it was the feature film, *Over the Brooklyn Bridge,* with Elliott Gould, Margaux Hemingway, and Sid Caesar.

Sarah was a busy young actress and model, but Rosellen always insisted that her school work come first. The rule was that if her grades went below an A-, she would have to stop working.

In those years before Sarah's career took off, she found time to be good at many other things. As a competitive figure skater, she finished in third place at the New York State regional competition. As one of the few girls studying tae kwon do, she earned a brown belt and placed fourth at a Madison Square Garden competition. She also loved photography, and persuaded her mom to build her a darkroom in the bathroom.

Sarah's daily routine was exhausting. She would start her day at the ice rink, then she

Before Sarah's TV career took off, she worked as a model and acted in more than 100 TV commercials.

would go to school. After school she would go to auditions and then go to tae kwon do. She was so busy that, by age 13, she was already wearing a pager.

Soon Rosellen realized that her daughter had taken on too many activities. One day she told Sarah, "You can pick two things, you can't do them all. And school has to be one of them." Sarah chose acting. Stage experience is very important for a serious actress to have, and at age nine, Sarah got her first chance to appear in a Broadway production. She appeared with Matthew Broderick and Eric Stoltz in *The Widow Claire.*

She made more movies, too. At age 11 she had a small role in the 1988 film *Funny Farm* with Chevy Chase, but for some reason she was never mentioned in the credits. In 1989 she appeared in *High Stakes.* It was the only time she acted under the name of just "Sarah Gellar."

She also continued to do both commercials and television shows. In 1981 she was on the sitcom *Love, Sidney,* with Tony Randall. In 1986 she appeared with Robert Urich on *Spenser: For Hire.* She reports, "He was just wonderful to me." Sarah even served briefly as cohost of a syndicated talk show for girls called *Girl Talk* in 1989.

Acting in front of thousands of people was easy for Sarah, but fitting in at her elementary school was a different story. She was always having to ask herself, "'Do I go to a school dance or slumber party or do I go to an audition?' I was always excluded from everything because I was different."

Sarah's junior-high experience was even worse. Because Sarah was bright and talented, and because, as she puts it, "everyone goes to private school in Manhattan," Sarah earned a partial scholarship to the exclusive Columbia Preparatory School. The other girls had rich parents and were mainly interested in lipstick and brand name clothes. Not Sarah—instead she concentrated on her studies.

You might think being an actress would

impress the other kids, but it didn't. Sarah said, "I never liked to talk about my acting, because if I did I was branded a snob, and if I didn't I was a still a snob. I would cry because I didn't understand why people didn't like me."

Not attending school for months at a time didn't help. At 13 years of age, she says, "I had more absences in the first month than you're supposed to have for an entire year. I was telling them I had back problems and had to go to the doctor all the time." Sarah had already moved to a new school when the television miniseries *A Woman Named Jackie* debuted. Now everyone could see where she had really been.

In this 1991 miniseries, for which she had to miss the eighth-grade trip to Busch Gardens, Sarah played a young Jackie Kennedy, and Roma Downey played Kennedy as an adult. Sarah thought Downey was so cool that she became the older actress's shadow all through the filming.

Sarah only lasted one month at her next school, LaGuardia, a place made famous by a film and television show called *Fame*. Sarah found that, although the school was dedicated to training young people who had talent, it didn't want students to go out and work until they graduated. When Sarah missed school to go to auditions, they threatened to fail her, even though she was getting straight A's.

In October 1992, Sarah finally found the right school for her. At the Professional Children's School she was with young "musicians from Julliard, dancers from the School of American Ballet, actors, writers, gymnasts, and some children of famous people." Here everyone came and went according to odd schedules,

so Sarah was no longer different. Actor Ryan Phillippe was one of her classmates.

Sarah briefly attended school at LaGuardia, seen here, a place made famous by the movie *Fame.* However, she found that the Professional Children's School was a better match for her busy work schedule.

This school experience was much better. Sarah went to parties, proms, and formals and had boyfriends. She admits, "Making out in parks is a very big thing to do in high school when you grow up in New York City. There was a playground right near my house and the swings saw a lot of action from me."

Sarah's career blossomed even before she finished her studies at the Professional Children's School.

DAYS: Julie Comes Home
Soap Opera
Magazine
AMC: Anton Reveals He And Kendall Are Lovers
Y&R Victor Pleads With Hope
GH Scott Flees Port Charles
B&B Ridge And Brooke Caught
ATWT: Behind The Scenes At Iva's Wedding

3

SOAP OPERA STAR

In 1991 Sarah auditioned for a part on a new afternoon television program to be called *Swans Crossing*. The show's creators, having noted how many young people watched adult "soap operas," had decided teens needed a "soap" of their own.

The term "soap opera" refers to a show that follows a serial format. Just a few tidbits of new information are given each day, and story lines can go on for years. This type of programming began in the days of silent movies when eight minutes was the longest film clip possible. As a result, directors shot many short episodes of larger stories.

When radio came along, daytime programming was largely ignored until 1930, when an Ohio schoolteacher named Irna Phillips came up with something new. She offered stay-at-home moms a family drama called *Painted Dreams*, and other shows of this kind quickly followed.

By the late 1930s an estimated 40 million people listened to these dramas. Who sponsored them? Mostly soap companies, so the shows themselves soon came to be called "soap operas" or just "soaps." The plots on those early shows would be considered tame by today's standards. *Ma Perkins*, for example, was about a kindly

---

Sarah became a soap star when she landed the role of Susan Lucci's daughter on *All My Children*.

grandmother who tried to take care of her extended family.

Modern soap operas are about heroines and romance, but they have adapted to fit a more modern audience. Alan Carter wrote in *Entertainment Weekly* that the modern soap is sustained by "backbiting, blackmail, and bed-hopping. [K]id characters on those shows have typically been ignored—or sent away to school at five only to reappear a few months later at 18, all grown up and ready for trouble."

The creators of *Swans Crossing* wanted to change all that. They focused on the love lives of 12 wealthy 14-year-olds in the fictional town of Swans Crossing. Rather than "the 3 Bs" mentioned above, these teens struggled with "2 Cs," crushes and crushed feelings.

Sarah, just 14 at the time, was happy to land the role of Sydney Rutledge on this new soap. Rich and spoiled, Sydney was the mayor's daughter who liked to manipulate people for her own purposes. "Sydney is kind of like the town witch," Sarah was quoted as saying.

Some people would probably rather play a heroine than a villainess, but not Sarah. Even then she realized that playing someone wicked can give an actress the chance to do outrageous things. An evil woman's reasons for her actions are usually complicated, calling for better and more varied acting skills.

Swans Crossing sounded like fun to Sarah because she would be able to work with kids her own age on story lines about things she understood. Better yet, being on a weekly series meant she got a weekly paycheck, and she and Rosellen needed the money. The show took a year to film and get on the air.

Meanwhile, Sarah got a part in a Neil Simon

In 1991, Sarah landed the part of Sydney Rutledge on the new teen soap opera *Swans Crossing*. Though the show was canceled after the first season, success on *All My Children* was soon to follow.

play called *Jake's Women.* In the play, a novelist named Jake has a series of mental conversations with the women who have been important in his life. They include his first and second wives, his daughter at different ages, his sister, a girlfriend, and his therapist. Sarah played "Molly," the novelist's then 12-year-old daughter. Everyone had high hopes for the play, but this time Simon's writing didn't go over as well, and *Jake's Women* closed.

Swans Crossing, too, was a disappointment, although it did have some loyal followers. The show's biggest downfall may have been its time slot. Although *Swans Crossing* was aimed at the 7 to 15 age group, most stations broadcast it at

2:00 P.M, when kids were still in school. *Swans Crossing* was canceled after the first season.

But just as her first regular job on television fizzled, Sarah heard about a casting call for a young actress to appear on *All My Children*. When Sarah went to audition for *All My Children*, she had no idea what kind of person "Kendall Hart" would be, but Sydney Rutledge had been a sweetheart compared to this girl. It was lucky for Sarah that she'd had so much practice being nasty in her previous role. That experience was about to pay off.

The casting department at *All My Children* intended to hire an older actress, but they had seen 14-year-old Sarah on *Swans Crossing*. They knew she could be convincing as a mean person, and she already had the reputation of being a professional. Sarah got the job.

Winning this role on *All My Children* was a huge break for her career. While *Swans Crossing* had been a new syndicated show with a limited audience, *All My Children*'s audience was estimated at 20 million. It had been on the air since 1970, so it was not about to be canceled in the near future.

The role of Kendall Hart was "as good as it gets" for a girl who liked to play nasty people. According to the plot line, when Kendall finally tells Erica that she is the child that Erica gave up years earlier, things really get strange. Kendall is so desperate to find her birth father, the one who raped Erica, that she convinces Erica's new husband, Dmitri, to help her. When Erica finds out about that, she kicks Kendall out of the house and tells Dmitri she wants a divorce.

Kendall repays Dimitri for his help by sleeping with a stable boy and telling everyone that

Sarah's brilliant portrayal of the hateful Kendall on *All My Children* endeared her to millions of soap opera fans. However, a turbulent relationship with the soap's star, Susan Lucci, led her to look for other acting opportunities in 1995.

Dmitri tried to rape her. Erica reacts by trying to stab Dmitri. She is then charged with attempted murder. On the witness stand, Erica says that she didn't mean to stab Dmitri; she just flipped out when she thought about the rape she suffered when she was 14. Finally Kendall admits she has been lying and goes to jail for perjury.

Sarah thought all this mayhem was great

fun, but she was a little squeamish about having to do a bedroom scene with a man who was much older than she. Luckily she and Michael Nader, who played Dmitri, were good friends. Also, they were both fully dressed under the covers, so Sarah was able to reassure herself that it was just a part of the job.

All My Children's fans loved watching the hateful Kendall, and overnight Sarah's face became familiar to millions. Total strangers would come up to her on the street and start talking. When she went to restaurants or hotels, she often got special treatment.

Once, at a movie theater, the ticket taker began to giggle when Sarah tried to enter. The theater manager came over to apologize, and he offered Sarah's group free admission and free treats from the concession stand. Sarah said, "It was the first time anyone had gone out of their way like that for me. He made us feel very special."

Sarah was quite happy on *All My Children*. In 1993 she told interviewer Michael S. Rush: "I thank Judy Wilson (*All My Children* 's casting director) so much for giving me the chance to actually be a teenager playing a teenager on the show."

When Terrie Collymore of *Soap Opera Digest* asked Sarah about her future in 1994, Sarah said, "As long as I have material I can sink my teeth into, I will continue to love what I'm doing. If that means staying at *All My Children* for the next 23 years, that's fine with me."

Shortly after that interview, Sarah's relationship with Susan Lucci appeared to go sour. Fan magazines reported that Lucci and Sarah hated each other, and Sarah did her best to squelch the rumors. She said that, although she and Lucci weren't close and didn't "do lunch," they did work well together. When Sarah won her Emmy in 1995, she also pointed out, "I won for scenes I submitted with her [Lucci]. You don't work alone—this was work we did together."

Sarah missed her prom, but she was able to take her new trophy to the after-prom party. A few weeks later, she graduated from high school with a perfect 4.0 average, even though she had completed her studies in just two and a half years. It was time to decide whether to go on to college or to devote all of her time to acting.

VAMPYR

4

BECOMING BUFFY

At age 18 Sarah decided she wanted to go on with her acting while her Emmy was still fresh in people's minds. Rosellen Gellar, on the other hand, had hoped her daughter would go to college. In the end, Rosellen reluctantly agreed to let Sarah have one year to find work in Hollywood.

It was soon obvious that Sarah's experience in daytime television meant little to casting departments in Los Angeles. For six months she pounded the pavement going from audition to audition. Over and over again she heard: "She's not ready," "She's too young," or "She's too 'soap.'"

Then Sarah's agent told her to go to Warner Brothers. This new television network had announced auditions for a potential show to be aimed at teens. Sarah was interested, but at first *Buffy the Vampire Slayer*'s title sounded like a joke. Then she learned that Joss Whedon, an Oscar nominee for coauthoring *Toy Story*, would be both the writer and director of the new show. Suddenly she wanted to know more about this project.

A little research revealed that Whedon's 1992 movie, also called *Buffy the Vampire Slayer*, had been funny, but it had bombed at the box office. According to *Time* magazine,

---

Buffy the Vampire Slayer made Sarah Michelle Gellar a mainstream TV star. The show became very popular with teens and young adults.

Whedon got the idea for the story from watching too many horror movies in which "bubblehead blonds wandered into dark alleys and got murdered by some creature." He later said in the book, *Buffy X-Posed*, "I began thinking that I would love to see a scene where a ditsy blond walks into a dark alley, a monster attacks her, and she kicks his [butt]. . . . I wanted to go for the thrills, the chills, and the action."

In Whedon's movie script, Buffy was never expected to be anything but pretty, but suddenly she is forced to learn how to deal with vampires. Although there are some funny lines, Whedon did not see his story primarily as comedy. Those in charge of actually making the movie saw things differently. When it came out, it was mostly funny, and Whedon was upset. He felt that his original script had been better than the final product, and several people at Warner Brothers agreed. They asked him to write some scripts for a possible television show.

When Sarah read a script for the television version of the story, she was impressed. She decided she had to play Buffy, and Whedon agreed to talk to her. But he told her, "You're really good, but you're not Buffy. You're Cordelia. So do you want to come in and test as Cordelia?" Sarah hesitated, then decided she did want to be part of his show, no matter who she played.

Sarah tested for Cordelia, and she got hired. The casting people definitely saw her as Cordelia, the snob, a character much like Kendall Hart. But the people at Warner Brothers can't be blamed too much for failing to see Buffy in the Sarah who tried out for them. This was before she became a blond, and those involved with the show had envisioned Buffy as a blond. Also, she

In 1995, Sarah tried out for the new TV show *Buffy the Vampire Slayer*, adapted from Joss Whedon's unsuccessful 1992 movie, *Buffy the Vampire Slayer*. Originally cast as the character Cordelia, she tried out for the role of Buffy and won the part.

remembers, "Both times [her first two auditions] I wore this ankle-length dress with sneakers, and they were afraid I had really bad legs."

Although Sarah was offered the part of Cordelia, she still begged to try out for Buffy. The casting people made her do five read-throughs and five screen tests before they reached a decision. When Sarah came out the last time, she was told, "We need you to read one more time." She reports, she started to cry and said, "You guys are wrecking me." She got dragged back in, and then everyone starting laughing. She had the part.

Maybe Sarah was in suspense for all this time, but Whedon claims she won him over much earlier. He wanted Buffy to be funny, tough, attractive, and weird; and Sarah could be all these things. "She gave us a reading that was letter-perfect and then she said, 'By the way . . . I did take tae kwon do for four years and I'm a brown belt. Is that good?'" What a question! Whedon was delighted to know that Sarah could do some of her own stunt work.

Charisma Carpenter was then hired as Cordelia, and she joined David Boreanaz, Nicholas Brendon, Anthony Head, and Sarah as the nucleus of the cast. Their first job was to put together a half-hour "presentation" that would sell *Buffy* to the executives at Warner Brothers. This was quite a challenge because Sarah and Anthony were the only experienced actors in the group. Furthermore, Whedon had never directed before, his support team was inexperienced, and their budget was very small for an action-oriented, special-effects program.

The resulting presentation was a little weak, but good enough to earn Whedon the green light to make 12 episodes of the show. The premiere was set for March 1997, and since this all happened in the spring of 1996, Whedon had enough time to fix what didn't work.

Whedon had to find someone to play Willow, Buffy's shy, computer-hacker friend. Dozens of young women read for the part until only two remained, Alyson Hannigan and another young actress from New Zealand. When Alyson read the script with Sarah and Nick, she had trouble pronouncing the computer terms. She was sure she had lost the part, but Whedon was impressed with how well she seemed to relate to the others. Adding Alyson to the cast made the chemistry between them all nearly perfect.

Now it was time for the players to make their characters come alive by bringing out all the individual quirks that Whedon had hinted at in the script. Perhaps Anthony Head had the easiest time of it. Being from England and having tons of experience in live stage productions, he found it a cinch to conquer Giles's very proper speech patterns and to sound clueless about American high-school students.

The other cast members faced bigger challenges. In Alyson's case, she had to let the audience know that a lot was going on under Willow's shy exterior, including a slightly loopy way of seeing the world. Nick had to find the perfect blend of sweetness, bravado, and insecurity for Xander. Charisma needed to make Cordelia both self-centered and caring at the same time.

David had the special requirement of convincing the viewers that Angel was 240 years old and never went out much during the day. He also needed to be just unusual enough so that audiences would believe him when he turned into a vampire before their eyes.

For Sarah, playing Buffy meant conveying the impression that she was both an outsider and a leader, a serious defender of the world as we know it, and a hip teenager. Then there were the unfamiliar slang words Whedon kept inventing for her to say. For example, the script for the first episode called for Sarah to come in and yell, "What's the 'sitch'?" She had no idea what "sitch" meant until Whedon explained that it was short for "situation."

Dealing with the subject of vampire slaying

David Boreanaz was cast as Angel, a 240-year-old vampire to play opposite Sarah Michelle Gellar's Buffy. Buffy the Vampire Slayer premiered on March 10, 1997.

was hard, too, because Sarah had an irrational fear of cemeteries and being buried alive. When a script called for her to be put in a grave, she told the producer, "Look, I can't do it, I'm sorry." But at 4:00 A.M. one morning she was forced to do the scene, and she cried all the way home. Gradually Sarah got so deeply into her rough-and-ready role that it got her into trouble on a visit to a popular amusement park. At one point in the day a fake vampire jumped out to scare the tourists, and Sarah gave the guy a karate chop.

As Sarah grew into her part, Whedon became more and more convinced that he had been right to cast her as Buffy. He said, "The show couldn't happen with anyone else. When Buffy's flighty or silly or addled, it's more charming because Sarah brings so much intelligence and depth to the character."

5

SCREAM QUEEN

The first half of the two-hour premiere of *Buffy the Vampire Slayer* was titled "Welcome to Hellmouth." The idea behind the whole show was that once in each generation, one girl in all the world is born to wage war against vampires.

Buffy is that girl. She's in a serious business, but she's also funny. When asked how one gets to be a vampire, Buffy says, "To make you a vampire they have to suck your blood. And then you have to suck their blood. It's like a whole big sucking thing."

But the vampire-slaying business can be a problem because no one understands you. As the show opens, Buffy has just been expelled from one school for wrecking the gym while fighting vampires. Now she is at Sunnydale High, hoping she can stay away from the "vamps," but no such luck. The school librarian tells her that Sunnydale sits right over Hellmouth, and vampires are everywhere.

In the second hour of the first show, the audience learns that, not only do the kids at her school fail to understand Buffy, but her mother is no better. We see Buffy in her room grabbing the stakes and equipment that she'll need to stop evil from conquering the world. Her mom tells

---

Buffy the Vampire Slayer premiered to good reviews in early 1997. Sarah's talent for playing Buffy helped her land roles in hit movies.

Buffy she can't go out that night, which upsets Buffy. Her mother sighs and says, "Everything is life and death when you're a 16-year-old." In Buffy's case, this is true!

All 12 of *Buffy*'s first season's episodes were shot before the first show went on the air. The final one, "Prophecy Girl," seemed to reflect writer/director Whedon's fears that *Buffy* might not live until fall. Buffy is killed in that episode, but later she is amazingly resurrected.

Warner Brothers embarked on a huge publicity campaign to launch the new show. While Sarah was doing some of these promotional appearances, she heard about an exciting new movie and decided to go for an audition. The day before *Buffy's* premiere, Sarah learned that she had landed a role in the movie, *I Know What You Did Last Summer.* So, instead of hanging around with the rest of the cast to worry about what the viewing public would think of their show, its star was on her way to a movie set in Southport, North Carolina.

Sarah didn't even see the premiere of *Buffy* on March 10, 1997, because no channel in Southport carried it. But Alyson Hannigan called her and happily reported that *Buffy* had scored the highest Nielsen rating ever for a Monday night show on the new WB (Warner Brothers) network.

The next time Alyson called, she was even more excited. She said, "Every time you go past a grocery store there's a *Buffy* billboard!" The show was getting great reviews, too. Tom Carson of the *Village Voice* wrote, "I can't think of a TV show that better captures how adolescence feels." *Time* magazine called it "the most talked-about show to have debuted in the past months." Claire Bickley of the *Toronto Sun* said,

"It's a big hoot; a cool, kicky, Junior *X-Files*." Tom Gliatto of *People* magazine had special praise for Sarah. He wrote, she played Buffy "with the right degree of put-upon resentment," and later added, this is "one of the brightest new shows of the season."

Meanwhile Sarah was working on the movie *I Know What You Did Last Summer*, her first starring role on the big screen. The movie was based on a popular young-adult novel written by Lois Duncan.

The 1973 novel is about four high school seniors who are in a car that hits an eight-year-old boy on a bicycle. The driver, a rich kid named Barry, doesn't want to stop because he's afraid the police will realize that he's been drinking. Barry's adoring friends, Helen and Ray, side with Barry, but Julie, Ray's girlfriend, is shocked at their attitude. The foursome leaves the scene of the accident, making it a hit-and-run, but they do make an anonymous call to report the incident. They all feel guilty when they hear the boy died.

A year later, when Julie gets a note saying, "I know what you did last summer," she panics. Soon, her three friends are getting notes, too, and Barry has a suspicious "accident." More scary events follow. In the book, the person revealed to be sending the notes makes perfect sense, and the ending is chilling but not bloody.

Kevin Williamson, who wrote the popular movie *Scream*, wrote the screen play for *I Know*, but he made major changes in Duncan's story. First, the person hit by the teens' car is an adult in a rain slicker, rather than a child. Second, instead of making an anonymous phone call to get help for the victim, these kids throw the body in the ocean. Third, the bad guy

In 1997, Sarah costarred with Ryan Phillippe, Jennifer Love Hewitt, and Freddie Prinze Jr. in the hit *I Know What You Did Last Summer*. It was her first big-screen role.

in the movie is a terrifying figure in a rain slicker who carries a meat hook. Fourth, lots of people are killed in bloody ways.

Sarah was chosen to be Helen. Ryan Phillippe played Barry, Jennifer Love Hewitt took the part of Julie, and Freddie Prinze Jr. was Julie's boyfriend Ray. The other stars were hired before Sarah was available and began working on the movie before she arrived. At her first day of rehearsal, Sarah was intimidated. She claims she called her manager and said, "I'm going to pack my bags because I'm going to get fired." But she didn't get fired, and she soon got the hang of playing Helen.

As the movie opens, Helen is on stage in a bathing suit winning the local beauty pageant. Sarah teased that appearing in a bathing suit was the scariest part of making this horror movie. Actually her biggest challenge was to shift from Buffy's "kick butt" mind-set to become the helpless Helen. Director Jim Gillespie had to tell her, "You can't hit the [bad] guy;" and he had to ask her not to run so fast. The next time they practiced her flight scene, Sarah left her shoes untied and put pebbles in them to make herself look clumsier. For the actual filming, her ankle-length gown and high heels helped slow her down.

It was a good thing the cast enjoyed each others' company, because there was no entertainment to be had in Southport after 9:00 P.M. Also, the town was less than thrilled to have a movie company monopolizing their space. Sarah told *Mr. Show Biz,* "They would close restaurants down when they saw us coming. People would decide to clean their boats and saw wood when we were filming, right next to the shoot."

While Sarah worried about the scary guy with the meat hook, *Buffy* was in more serious danger. For a time it looked as though the show would be canceled due to its low ratings. Although its premiere was the highest rated show for the new WB network, *Buffy* was the 100th out of 107 programs rated by Nielsen. Warner Brothers wisely decided to give *Buffy* time to grow on viewers. The *X-Files* first year's ratings had been horrible, too, and it later became a powerhouse for the FOX network.

Sarah was relieved to hear that *Buffy* would be renewed and equally happy when Kevin Williamson offered her a part in another movie. Since his *Scream* had become the biggest grossing horror movie of all time, Miramax wanted a sequel. Halfway through filming *I Know,* he offered Sarah a small part in *Scream 2.*

She was eager to be in a movie that was almost certain to be a hit and excited to think about working with Neve Campbell and Courteney Cox. But there was one problem: Sarah had never actually seen the original *Scream.* So she, Charisma Carpenter, and Alyson Hannigan went to see Williamson's blockbuster together.

Sarah was impressed that the first movie and the script for the sequel contained more than just mindless violence. The characters in both were brave and felt real; the plots took interesting turns. The director for both, Wes Craven, obviously knew his business, so Sarah agreed to head to Atlanta as soon as she finished shooting *I Know.*

In *Scream 2* Sarah plays a college student. As the story opens, the serial killings in the first movie have been made into a movie named *Stab.* During that movie's preview, two of Sarah's fellow students are brutally killed.

Sarah's first scene shows her in a film class discussing the murders. One of her classmates believes that the movie's subject matter was directly responsible for what happened. "That's so 'moral majority,'" Sarah's character Cici counters. "You can't blame real-life violence on entertainment." Cici might not have been so quick to say this had she known she would be the next one targeted by the killer.

After *Scream 2* was released, people in real life began to dispute Cici's statement. A 16-year-old boy in California stabbed his mother to death with the help of his two cousins. It was said the trio had planned to wear Grim Reaper masks and use voice distortion boxes just like the killers in the *Scream* movies. The real-life teens, however, failed to come up with the money to buy the masks.

Sarah continued to defend Cici's point of

Sarah starred with Neve Campbell and Courteney Cox in *Scream 2*. Even though her movie career was taking off, Sarah still remained dedicated to *Buffy the Vampire Slayer*.

view. She said, "It's horrible, but these people should know better. Murder is wrong; people know that. We don't say, 'Do this.' We are entertaining you. Not everything is a public-service announcement."

Scream 2's director had just as much trouble slowing Sarah down as her director did on *I Know*. Craven told her, "Don't kill the bad man, because then he can't come back for a sequel."

Since Cici was a minor character in the movie, Sarah wasn't in Atlanta long, but she thought working for Craven was interesting. She reported that he hid people around the set in order to get honest reactions of surprise from his actors and that no one saw the final pages of the script until a few days before they were filmed.

When Sarah was done filming *Scream 2*, she returned to California to tape the fall episodes of *Buffy the Vampire Slayer*. Whedon and the rest of the cast welcomed her with open arms because up until that point they had only been able to film scenes that she wasn't in.

6

SUCCESS AND CONTROVERSY

Now that *Buffy the Vampire Slayer* had an established reputation, Whedon and the cast vowed not to disappoint their audience. New characters like Spike and Drusilla, the coolest vampire team ever, were added, and returning characters formed new relationships.

Viewers wanted Buffy and Angel to become more important to each other, and by the show's Halloween episode, the slayer was obviously attracted to the brooding vampire with a soul. That show earned a 3.7 Nielsen rating, *Buffy's* best numbers so far.

The November 17th script sent the two on their first date. This was an especially fun assignment for Sarah because Angel took her ice skating. She finally had a chance to show off the skills she had worked so hard to learn in New York.

Then on January 19, 1998, Whedon abandoned his earlier policy of not having intimate scenes in the show. Buffy and Angel became lovers, and the results were shocking and horrific. Because of an ancient gypsy curse, one night of bliss for Angel caused him to lose his soul again and become the evil Angelus.

This complete turnaround in Angel's behavior was

Buffy's romance with the vampire Angel, played by actor David Boreanaz, was very popular with fans of the show. In real life, Sarah and David are close friends.

traumatic for Buffy and equally hard on Sarah in real life. She told Jean Cummings of the science fiction magazine *Starburst*, "The scariest thing we've done is when Angel went bad. . . . [David Boreanaz is] . . . like kind of an older brother to me. . . . [U]sually we're pals, holding hands and hugging but we couldn't at this point because he was doing these horrible things to me and he would just make me cry and cry, but then he would hold me, and I remembered that this is David, not a monster. But it was hard to figure out where the line ended sometimes."

As the filming for *Buffy*'s 1997-98 season went on, the movies she had made the summer before had their premieres, and suddenly everyone could see what good career moves they had been. *I Know What You Did Last Summer* opened to huge crowds and grossed $16 million dollars in its first weekend. Six months later, it had earned over $70 million. *Scream 2*, which opened in December, made more money in its first weekend than the other top nine films combined.

Suddenly, Sarah's agent was besieged by people wanting to interview her. Jay Leno and David Letterman invited her to be on their shows, and she was offered many movie scripts. On January 17, 1998, she hosted the television show *Saturday Night Live* to rave reviews. In March she won a Blockbuster Entertainment Award for Best Supporting Actress in the horror film category for her role in *I Know What You Did Last Summer.*

Buffy the Vampire Slayer's second season ended with Buffy being forced to kill Angelus, the bad version of Angel. This was the year that David left to star in his own show called

With the huge success of *I Know What You Did Last Summer* and *Scream 2*, Sarah was offered many movie scripts. Here she is in *Simply Irresistible*, released in 1999.

Angel. When Whedon first told Sarah that David and Charisma would be leaving to do a spin-off, she felt happy for them, but she also cried. Maybe that's one reason Whedon scheduled those two-hour "events" where the cast came together again.

Sarah, too, went on with her life and her movie career. Her next starring role was in a romantic movie called *Simply Irresistible* that was filmed mostly in New York City at Brindel's Department Store. In this movie she plays a sweet, average young restaurant owner whose business is failing until a magic crab and Sean Patrick Flanery come to her rescue.

The movie should have been charming with a copper-haired Sarah wearing glamorous clothes and smiling more than she ever could as Buffy. But the film that got made was less irresistible than its script had been. The idea of the crab being her guardian angel was mostly lost in the translation from script to film, and her love scenes with Flanery were duds. Leah Rozen of *People* magazine said, "Together, these two have about as much zing as cornstarch." The movie came out in October 1999 and was Sarah's first failure at the box office.

Sarah quickly recovered her reputation for appearing in winners with the second movie she made in the summer of 1998. Sarah had read the script for *Cruel Intentions* much earlier and thought it would be a great change of pace for her.

She begged writer/director Roger Kumble to let her play the evil Kathyrn. At first he couldn't picture her as a villainess, but some old footage of her as Kendall Hart on *All My Children* was enough to convince him she could be horrifying.

Still, Kumble urged Sarah to think twice about accepting the role. He pointed out that everyone loved her so much as Buffy that this would be a big career risk. Sarah said she had to play this part. She told Krumble, "If I waited any longer to show people I could stretch as an actor, it probably would be too late because no one would want to see me in anything other than a Buffy role."

Eventually, Kumble hired Sarah to play the role of Kathryn and cast Ryan Phillippe as her equally evil stepbrother, Sebastian. Both actors were glad that they had been friends since high school, because they had to appear to be very intimate in the movie.

Sarah's character in *Cruel Intentions* was horribly foulmouthed. Also, one scene required her to kiss another woman. Trying to pull that off in New York's Central Park with hundreds of onlookers gawking was not her idea of a good time.

The R-rated story line concerns the viciously cruel wager Kathryn and Sebastian make over whether or not they can wreck the lives of two of the nicest girls in the neighborhood. Sarah let her blond hair go back to its natural brunette to match Kathryn's dark personality and dived into her part. Director Kumble later told the *Chicago Tribune*, "She unquestionably is the most professional actor I've ever worked with."

Sarah also did a voice-only part as a Gwendy doll in Warner Brothers' 1998 fantasy film, *Small Soldiers*.

In the fall of 1998, Angel returned from the dead to help *Buffy*'s ratings soar. He still appeared evil at times, but Buffy was confident he loved her. When Angel was shot with a poison arrow in the final episode and had to have someone's blood to survive, it was Buffy that kept him alive.

The end of the season was marked by controversy. An episode called "Earshot," slated to be aired on April 26, had Buffy reading the thoughts of some kids who planned to gun down their classmates. Just a few days earlier, a real-life massacre happened at Columbine High in Colorado, and network executives decided that the episode of Buffy shouldn't be run at that time. They refused to allow "Earshot" to be seen until September.

The second half of the season finale, the one about the "blood transfusion," was also pulled from its original viewing date of May 25. This one had the town's mayor turning into a gigantic lizard and sending out demons to kill the student body. "Graduation Day Part 2" was finally shown on July 13, 1999.

The summer of 1999 found Sarah taking a well-deserved vacation, at least that was what she called it. She began with two weeks in New York City, where she again served as host of *Saturday Night Live.* While she was there she got tickets to the newest *Star Wars* movie courtesy of George Lucas, whose daughter is a big fan of *Buffy.*

From New York, she flew to the Dominican Republic to help Habitat for Humanity build a house. The final part of that trip was in the copilot's seat of a tiny prop jet. Sarah had always been a white-knuckled flyer, but she faced her fears and even took over the plane's controls for awhile.

In the Dominican Republic, Sarah worked at stirring cement and getting it to the construction site. But she was able to help Habitat for Humanity even more with the publicity she brought to their project.

Teen People magazine wanted an interview, and Sarah convinced them to do it at the construction site in the Dominican Republic. Yolanda Perez Aria, a poor, single mother, and the glamorous Hollywood star, Sarah, hit it off. When Sarah finished her work, she stepped out of the tennis shoes she was wearing and left them for Yolanda's daughter as a present.

In August 1999 Sarah signed a contract with Maybelline and began to shoot commercials for cosmetics.

The fall 1999 season of *Buffy the Vampire Slayer* found Buffy and Willow enrolled in college, and Buffy got a new boyfriend named Riley. Ongoing plots revolved around a new slayer named Faith, and Riley, Angel, and Buffy making each other jealous and engaging in lots of romantic entanglements.

Up until this season Sarah had never questioned Joss Whedon's writing, but now she

Sarah hosted *Saturday Night Live* for the first time in the summer of 1999.

found the courage to tell him some doubts she had about the story line. She pointed out places where she felt that Faith wouldn't have acted the way Whedon had her acting. He listened, and a few changes were made.

Sarah's summer project for 2000 was the movie *Harvard Man.* James Toback, who wrote the screenplay based on his own experiences in the 1960s, had asked Sarah to be in his movie several years earlier, and she had agreed. It took him five years to get the filming scheduled, but

In 2000, Sarah won the MTV Movie Award for Best Female Performance for her role as Kathryn Merteuil in the 1999 movie *Cruel Intentions.*

he said that once he had a star like Sarah on board, he felt certain the movie would get made.

In *Harvard Man,* which Toback also directs, Sarah stars as a young Harvard philosophy professor who has an affair with a student basketball player. Her character Cindy Bandolini is also the daughter of a crime boss, and she encourages her lover to fix a game for the mob. The film was filmed mostly in Toronto and the cast included Adrian Grenier, Rebecca Gayheart,

Joey Lauren Adams, Eric Stoltz, and NBA player Ray Allen. It was scheduled to premiere in the summer of 2001.

In August, Sarah returned to Hollywood and began filming the 2000-2001 season of *Buffy the Vampire Slayer.* A new face on the show that season was Buffy's little sister, "Dawn," played by Michelle Trachtenberg of *Harriet the Spy* fame. Since Dawn just appeared in the opening episode with no explanation of where she had been all these years, fans were understandably confused. Some even felt their intelligence had been insulted. They pointed out that, after watching the show for four seasons, they would have known if Buffy had a younger sister. They hoped Joss Whedon would eventually explain it all. At the time this book was written, he hadn't offered an explanation.

7 BEYOND BUFFY

Sarah Michelle Gellar is much more than just a pretty blonde who slays vampires. She enjoys her time off from work, and sometimes can be found driving her Land Rover off-road. She owns a beautiful new house, which she cleans with the help of a maid who comes every other week. She has two Maltese terriers named Thor and Tyson, plus an impressive collection of first-edition children's books. She claims Dr. Suess as her favorite author because of the line "There's a gellar in the cellar" in his book *There's a Wocket in My Pocket*.

When Sarah goes out, it's often to Starbucks for a vanilla ice blend or to get sushi. But going out means she must avoid autograph seekers and reporters, so Sarah likes to invite friends over to her house for barbecues. These people include the gang from *Buffy* and others she's worked with in movies and on television. Melissa Joan Hart (*Sabrina the Teenage Witch*) and Jenna von Oy, who starred in a television show called *Blossom*, are apt to drop by. Brittany and Ashley, close friends from Sarah's school days, visit often. And her special friend is Freddie Prinze Jr., who she began calling "my baby" back in 1997 when they were filming *I Know What You Did Last Summer* together.

Sarah continued to star in *Buffy the Vampire Slayer* for the 2000-2001 season. Here she is pictured with Freddie Prinze Jr., her close friend and costar in *I Know What You Did Last Summer*.

Her friends agree that Sarah talks a mile a minute and likes to manage everyone else's life. But they are quick to add that she's caring, funny, and smart, so smart that the advice she gives them is usually worth following.

What lies ahead for Sarah? The possibilities are endless for this talented and "together" young actress. Of course, she'll continue to star each week on *Buffy* and to take on new movies that interest her. Maybe she'll even do more films for Kevin Williamson, who was impressed by how hard she worked for him. He said of Sarah, "You know when you hire her to do a job she's not going to be in the trailer, complaining about everything. She's going to be right out there at three in the morning, barefoot, in the freezing cold, giving you the 10th take."

She has to appear in more advertisements for Maybelline. More magazines want her on their covers, and more talk show hosts are asking her for interviews. Every day thousands of fans check out hundreds of websites for information on where to see more of Sarah and where to buy dozens of items bearing her picture.

As one of the most downloaded Hollywood stars on the Internet, Sarah has mixed feelings about the web. She is quick to agree that all of those chat rooms really helped *Buffy the Vampire Slayer* grow to be as popular as it has. But a website also sold her home address and fake pictures of her have been posted.

Being a Hollywood star can be scary at times, and Sarah knows she must take the good with the bad. She will continue to do what it takes to follow her dreams as long as she can be true to herself at the same time. And those dreams will no doubt change as she grows as an actress and as a person.

Among other projects, Sarah starred in a popular ad campaign for Maybelline. Here she is at the 2000 Teen Choice Awards.

Joss Whedon, who knows Sarah as well as anyone, offers this observation: "Sarah has been [acting] her whole life. And that could make a person completely strange and . . . stupid. But Sarah thinks about the whole picture. She could direct. She could produce. She could do all those things very ably. She's as good an actress as I've ever worked with."

Only time will tell what new demons Sarah will slay and what new worlds she will conquer.

Chronology

1977 Born in New York City on April 14 to Steven and Rosellen Gellar

1981 Discovered by a talent agent at a restaurant

1982 Did series of Burger King commercials

1983 Appeared in the television movie *An Invasion of Privacy*

1984 Appeared in movie *Over the Brooklyn Bridge*

1986 Appeared in the television series *Spenser: For Hire*

1987 On Broadway in *The Widow Claire*

1988 Appeared in movie *Funny Farm*

1989 Appeared in movie *High Stakes* as "Sarah Gellar;" hosted television show *Girl Talk*

1991 Appeared in television mini-series *A Woman Named Jackie*

1992 Starred in television series *Swans Crossing*; appeared off-Broadway in *Jake's Women*; began attending the Professional Children's School

1993 Began three-year run on *All My Children*

1994 Nominated for first Emmy

1995 Won an Emmy

1996 Moved to Los Angeles

1997 Began starring role in TV series *Buffy the Vampire Slayer*; starred in movies *I Know What You Did Last Summer* and *Scream 2*; starred in TV movie *Beverly Hills Family Robinson*

1998 Won Blockbuster Award for *I Know What You Did Last Summer*; hosted *Saturday Night Live*; starred in movies *Simply Irresistible* and *Cruel Intentions*

1999 Hosted *Saturday Night Live*; signed contract with Maybelline

2000 Filmed *Harvard Man*

2001 Engaged to actor Freddie Prinze Jr.

ACCOMPLISHMENTS

Television

1983 *An Invasion of Privacy* (movie)

1989 *Girl Talk*

1991 *A Woman Named Jackie* (mini-series)

1992 *Swans Crossing*

1993 *All My Children*

1997 *Buffy the Vampire Slayer*
Beverly Hills Family Robinson (movie)

Films

1984 *Over the Brooklyn Bridge*

1988 *Funny Farm* (uncredited)

1989 *High Stakes*

1997 *I Know What You Did Last Summer*
Scream 2

1998 *Small Soldiers* (voice only)

1999 *She's All That* (uncredited)
Simply Irresistible
Cruel Intentions

2001 *Harvard Man*
The It Girl

Stage

1987 *The Widow Claire*

1992 *Jake's Women*

Awards

1995 Daytime Emmy Award: Outstanding Younger Leading Actress

1998 Blockbuster Entertainment Award: Favorite Supporting Actress

1999 Saturn Award: Best Genre TV Actress

2000 MTV Movie Award: Best Female Performance; Best Kiss

FURTHER READING

Baker, Jennifer. *Sarah Michelle Gellar*. New York: Simon & Schuster, 1998.

Golden, Christopher and Nancy Holder. *Buffy the Vampire Slayer: Sunnydale High Yearbook*. New York: Pocket Books, 1999.

Laslo, Cynthia. *Sarah Michelle Gellar.* New York: Children's Press, 2000.

Stafford, Nikki. *Bite Me! Sarah Michelle Gellar and Buffy the Vampire Slayer.* Toronto: ECW, 1998.

Powell, Phelan. *Sarah Michelle Gellar.* Bear, Delaware: Mitchell Lane, 2001.

ABOUT THE AUTHOR

MARILYN D. ANDERSON was born and raised on a dairy farm in Minnesota. For 17 years she taught music in Minnesota, Vermont, and Indiana. She has written 21 children's books and dozens of magazine articles. Some of her most popular books are *Come Home Barkley*, *The Bridesmaid Wears Track Shoes*, and *Hot Fudge Pickles*.

Index

PHOTO CREDITS:

2: Photofest
6: Burstein/Globe Photos
9: Photofest
11: Ed Gellar/Globe Photos
14: Ed Gellar/Globe Photos
18: Burstein/Globe Photos
21: Michael S. Yamashita/Corbis
22: Burstein/Globe Photos
25: Photofest
27: Photofest
30: Photofest
33: Photofest
36: Lisa Rose/Globe Photos
38: Lisa Rose/Globe Photos
42: Photofest
45: Photofest
46: Photofest
49: Photofest
53: Henry McGee/Globe Photos
54: Fitzroy Barrett/Globe Photos
56: Sara Jaye/Globe Photos
59: Kelly Jordan/Globe Photos

Cover photo: Victor Malafronte/Archive Photos